Show and Tell

A Primer for Self-Publishers

Ruth Hagopian • Cathleen O'Brien • Julie Thompson

HOT off the PRESS
BOOKS

San Francisco • California

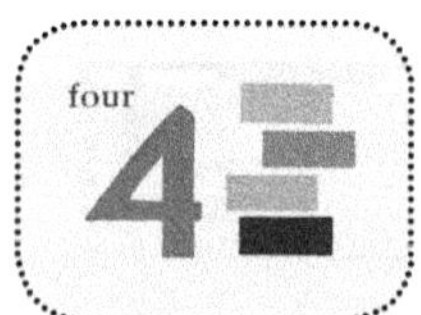

Dedication

To all those who want to get that book out of their heads and into readers' hands.

ISBN: 13: 978-0615568027

Designed by A Book in the Hand
San Francisco, California
abookinthehand.com

HOT off the PRESS
BOOKS

Published by
Hot off the Press Books
hotoffthepressbooks.com

Table of Contents

Unit 2

DESIGN: *Cut, Paste and Color* 34

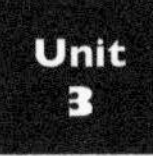

MARKETING: *Make Some Noise* 60

Introduction

Books, whether hardback, paperback, eBook or PDF, are still the best way to get your message out to a larger audience. In the business world, books are practically the new business card.

But how can self-publishers make their books as professional as those from major publishers?

First, write a book proposal. This handy document and the research involved in putting it together, are the blueprint you will use to build your book. It also helps you establish why your book is needed in the marketplace, and what makes it unique.

Then, get your brain dump (aka rough draft) on the page. Once that's done, you're ready for the real work of writing a book: rewriting and editing.

Familiarize yourself with the basics of good book design, including the front and back cover and interior layout. You may not design your book yourself, but you should know what types of things make a book look professional, and which scream amateur.

It's a shame to put all that work into your book simply to see it die on the vine because you don't have a marketing plan. Marketing starts with the book proposal, as you consider your ideal readers and how to reach them. It continues throughout the process and goes into high gear when your book is published.

Show and Tell: A Primer for Self-Publishers is an easy-to-digest set of tips that take your book from blah to ta-da! Sometimes, a little bit of good advice really does go a long way. We look forward to reading your book.

Ruth, Cathleen and Julie

Unit 1

Editing

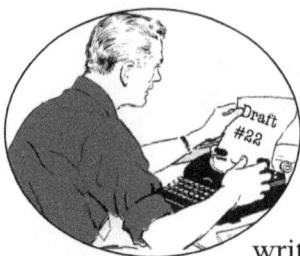

Playing with Words

Many people who want to write a book are prevented from doing so because they're not writers. They get stalled and stymied, but guess what? Professional writers do, too. Remember, if you have something to say, it's worth the effort.

If you want to create a unique book, your expertise and point of view are the most important ways to make your book stand out.

To get it down on paper, you have two choices: Either plow through it on your own or get help. If you try to do it yourself and get overwhelmed, hire a writer, content editor or writing coach to work with you. It's far better to use her expertise to get your project on track, than leave your book in the eternal to-do pile.

Now is not the time to overthink how much time it will take or how well your book will be received. Think about setting up a place to work where you can write regularly with your reference books, music, snacks — whatever inspires or helps you stay on task. Breathe. Relax into your own creative process.

Don't edit as you write. To paraphrase writer Anne Lamott, give yourself permission to write a shitty first draft. Get your thoughts down on the page and then start shaping them into polished prose. The work is worth the reward: a professionally published book with your name on the cover.

SHOW

Thanks for making those suggestions for my table of contents!

Get Organized

Creating a table of contents is the first step in organizing your book. This will serve as a map to guide your writing, help you decide if the sections and chapters are in the right order, and know if you've left out any important information.

Think about the main topics you want to write about. One section in a dog book might cover breeds, training and keeping your dog healthy. Another section might be about traveling with your dog and include pet-friendly locations, what to pack for Fido and emergency care on the road. Once these broad areas are figured out, it's much easier to fill in the chapters

SHOW

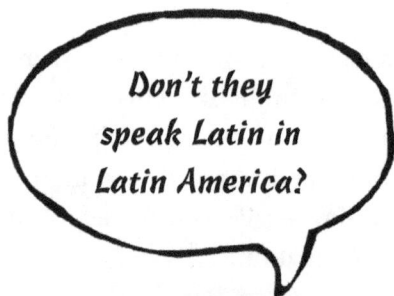

Says Who?

Don't guess. Don't assume. Don't be lazy with the facts. Just because you read it somewhere or found it online doesn't make it true.

Find reliable sources and fact check your manuscript. It gives you and your book more integrity, credibility and authority.

DUNCE
Wasn't it
Shakespeare
who said,
*"Never trust everything
you read on
the Internet?"*

SHOW

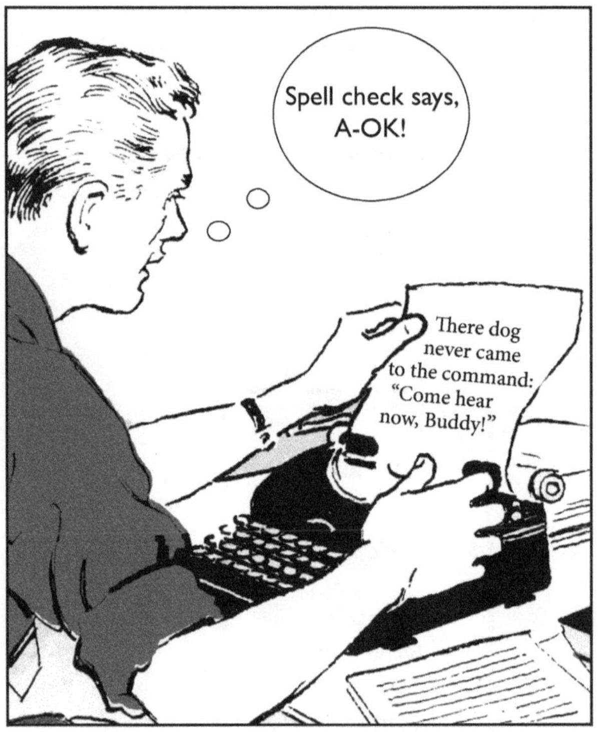
Spell check says, A-OK!
There dog never came to the command: "Come hear now, Buddy!"

The Devil's in the Details

Besides a poorly designed cover, nothing shouts amateur louder than misspellings and typos. Don't make them.

Use spell check but don't rely on it, since 'there' and 'here' are spelled correctly and won't be flagged, but don't have the same meaning as 'their' and 'hear.'

How do you avoid looking foolish? Read, read and re-read. Read your work from back to front so misspellings jump out at you. Hire an editor to proof your work. Read it one more time.

homework

Look up the definitions of these words:
affect and effect
farther and further
that and which
Always use them correctly!

SHOW

Don't: *Each man had their book.*

Do: *Each man had his book.*

Don't: *People that write are more fun.*

Do: *People who write are more fun.*

Grammar School

Grammatical mistakes can be tougher to catch than typos, but are just as important to correct. For many, the problem is not knowing the rule. Now that you're a writer, invest in a professional resource like the *Chicago Manual of Style* or the *AP Stylebook*.

Then use it!

A Note from our Editor

Don't forget how important the placement of a comma can be. You wouldn't want to rewrite history by saying, "Lincoln wrote The Gettysburg Address while traveling on the back of an envelope."

SHOW

Don't

Marilyn calmly read her book, not realizing her kitchen was on FIRE!!!

Do

Marilyn calmly read her book, not realizing her kitchen was on fire!

Less is More

You know Aunt Ida? The one who gets (the wrong kind of) attention by wearing sparkly blue eye shadow and a micromini skirt? Overuse of capitals, bolds, underlines and exclamation points is the literary equivalent.

Style Makeover Tips:

• Don't bold, capitalize and underline the same word. Pick one.

• One exclamation point is sufficient. Really!

• Don't be a hyperlink tease. On the web, underlines indicate a link, and since most books have an eBook version and online excerpts, underlines that are not links confuse the reader. Whenever you consider an underline, italics would probably be better.

SHOW

Emily's Organic Restaurant
Today's Specials
"Fresh" milk
"Beef" Bourguignon
"Real" Eggs

Would you eat here?

"Stop Doing This"

Quotation marks for anything other than dialogue are only used when something is ironic. If we had a nickel for every time we've seen quotation marks used incorrectly, well, we'd have a lot of nickels.

Just say what you mean. If Betty is your best friend, say she's your best friend. If you can't stand her, then feel free to refer to Betty as your "best" friend.

SHOW

Do

files:
Dog Book2RH
Dog Book1JT
The Big Dog Book

Don't

files:
My Edits
New Version
The Big Dog Book

Version Control

Have we mentioned you'll be doing a lot of rewriting? Save yourself a ton of grief by having a logical naming and filing scheme for your work. Every time you open a file to write or edit, do a "Save As" and give the file a new name.

Make the name sequential by including either a number or date. If you're writing with someone else, add your initials after the number or date, and make sure they do the same.

Keep older versions in their designated file, and show only the most recent version on your desktop, so you can find it quickly.

SHOW

GO TO
JAIL
You did not get permission
to use all the lyrics to the
Beatles' song, "Help!"

Ask First

Including all or part of someone else's published work in your book, whether it's text, a song lyric or a poem, without their consent is a no-no. Get written permission from the copyright holder as soon as possible.

Yes, this step can be a pain and may take a while, but on the plus side, you show respect for other writers and artists, and just might avoid a lawsuit.

I didn't know you couldn't go on the Internet, find a beautiful photograph and use it for the cover of your book.

SHOW

Don't

I think that there are so many very exciting cities to visit, but San Francisco is the best. My all-time favorite place is by far Golden Gate Park because it has tons and tons of super beautiful things to see there.

Do

San Francisco is an exciting city, and my favorite spot is Golden Gate Park.

Write Tight

If you can delete a word or phrase without changing the meaning of your sentence, delete it.

Using excess words and statements might be how you talk, but shouldn't be how you write. Go through your manuscript and cut extra words that aren't descriptive or don't move your ideas along.

Finding your writer's voice is one thing. Rambling on is another. Learn the difference.

homework

Read James Joyce.
Now read Gertrude Stein.

How are they different?

4+

Review: Playing with Words

Write a short consise first sentence.

The printer's bid was thorough and affordable.

Use a thesaurus to find a synonym for each word.

Delicious: Scrumptious

Comprehensive: Exhaustive

Beautiful: Beguiling

See Jane proofread.

See Dick rewrite.

Underline the correct word.

The old dog took (its, it's) time.

At 3 p.m., (its, it's) time for tea.

I'll do anything (accept, except) that.

I cannot (accept, except) that gift.

The scarf (complemented, complimented) his green eyes.

Thank you for the (complement, compliment).

Unit 2

Design

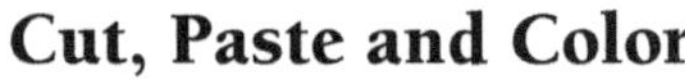

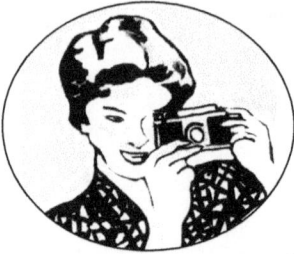

Cut, Paste and Color

Word-of-mouth advertising has a huge influence on book sales. But someone has to first plunk down some cash, buy a copy and get the ball rolling. The single best way to do this (unless you're famous like Barack Obama or Snooki), is with a strong cover design. Strong means your cover, a) gets the reader's attention, b) conveys the type of book you've created and, c) reflects your writing style.

Pretty tall order, eh?

As one of your strongest marketing tools, your book cover should be created by someone who not only understands good design aesthetics, but also knows how to sell books. The same goes for the back cover. Don't blindly choose an online template and cross your fingers, hoping for the best. Do your homework.

Layout design (inside the book) is also hugely important. Your self-published book, at first glance, should have the same quality as those produced by major publishers. The typefaces, page layout, headers and other elements will give a professional polish (or not) to your manuscript. It's like housekeeping. You take it for granted when it's done well, but most certainly notice when it's done poorly.

Our design pro says the secret of good design is to simplify. Whether your book is full of words, pictures or both, don't clutter the page with too many design elements that get in the reader's way.

Also avoid ornate typefaces. They're hard to read and distract from your intent.

For more gems from the book design treasure trove, read on.

SHOW

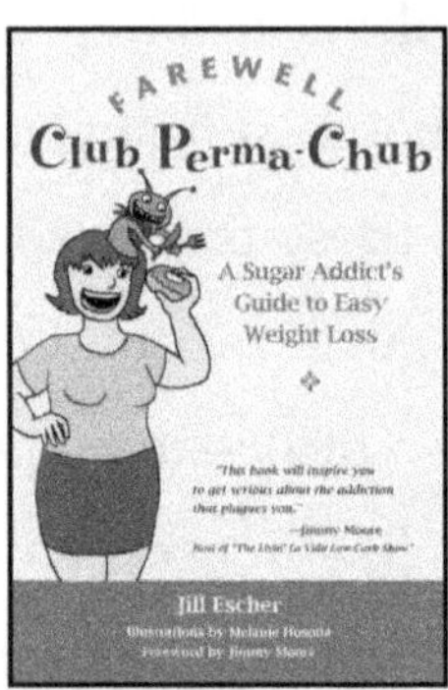

PORTRAIT

Self-help

Cookbooks

Novels

Memoirs

LANDSCAPE

Art/Photography

Commemorative

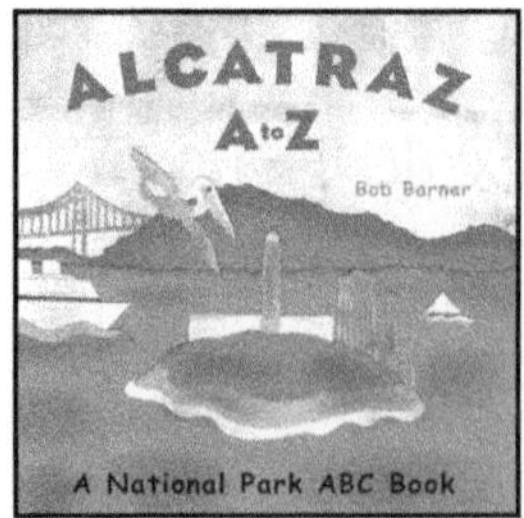

SQUARE FORMAT

Children's Books

Humor

Novelty

Size Matters

Until all books become digital, choosing a book size is important. But don't overthink it. Publishers have spent ages figuring out what book sizes work best, so why not use their expertise and match your book's genre with industry standards.

Text paperbacks are generally 5" x 8" and 6" x 9" (or close variations). These sizes work well for fiction, nonfiction, business, how-to and self-help books.

Bump up the size for art and photography books to 7 1/2" x 9" or 8 1/2" x 11" and you'll have more space for larger pictures and two or three columns of type. Square books are fun, modern and also a good way to combine images and text.

homework

Go through your house and count how many vertical, landscape and square books you have.

Which format is most popular?

SHOW

Serif fonts

ABCDEFGHIJKLMNOPQRSTUVWXYZ

The brown dog ran down the street.

Sans serifs fonts

ABCDEFGHIJKLMNOPQRSTUVWXYZ

The brown dog ran down the street.

FUN fonts

ABCDEFGHIJKLMNOPQRSTUVWXYZ

The brown dog ran down the street.

Fun with Fonts

Like too many cooks in the kitchen, too many typefaces in your book can really create a mess.

Serif fonts, like Times and Garamond, have little feet on the end of the strokes. They are considered easier to read and are most often used for body copy.

Sans serif fonts, like Helvetica and Futura, are best for titles, headlines, subheads, captions, charts and graphics.

DUNCE
My computer has 3,455 typefaces. Why can't I use all of them. Wouldn't that look pretty?

S H O W

Tom was telling a story about a picture. The other boys and girls wanted to be polite to him. They tried to be good listeners. It is very hard to be a good listener because it means you actually have to listen to what the other person is saying!

VOWELS

Do you know the vowels? The are a, e, i, o, u, and sometimes w and y. In pronouncing words, remember vowels are very important letters.

CONSONANTS

All the other letters in the alphabet are consonants. Consonants are cool, but vowels are more cool.

Can you pronounce these groups of consonants?

s_ck c_t fr_g

Don't Leave Us Hanging

Never end a paragraph with one word (called a widow). Bring down one or two words from the previous line to keep her company.

Never end a page with a new section headline. Add space to push it to the next column or page.

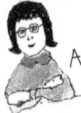

A Note from our Designer

Lately, I've been noticing neglected widows in books from major publishing houses! Are widows the new swinging single gals?

SHOW

THE SEVEN
DEADLY SINS

LUST
GLUTTONY
GREED
SLOTH
WRATH
ENVY
PRIDE

People at the Party

BOYS GIRLS

"Never eat more than you can lift."

—Miss Piggy

Eye Candy

If your book has many photos and illustrations, keep the rest of the design simple so they'll stand out.

You can break up a text-heavy page with pull quotes; those enlarged juicy bits of text that grab your readers' attention and convince them to dive into the chapter.

Or try snappy subheads to accent the page. You might even consider dingbats (the fun symbols, not your cousin Earl) in place of bullet points for variety.

You don't have to use graphic illustrations, but if you do, make sure they're placed throughout the book in balance with the text.

SHOW

This leading is too big

This leading is too big

This leading is too big

This leading is too big

This leading is too big

This leading is too small
This leading is too small
This leading is too small
This leading is too small
This leading is too small
This leading is too small
This leading is too small
This leading is too small

This leading is just right
This leading is just right
This leading is just right
This leading is just right
This leading is just right
This leading is just right
This leading is just right

Space to Breathe

Make reading your book an enjoyable experience by choosing type that's not too small or too large.

Also, pay attention to the space between the lines, which is called leading. If there's too little space or too much, it's hard to read and no fun. In fact, leading is as important for readability as the type itself.

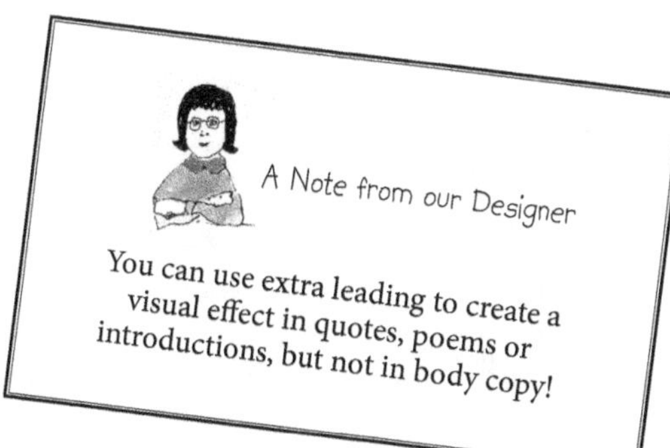

A Note from our Designer
You can use extra leading to create a visual effect in quotes, poems or introductions, but not in body copy!

SHOW

Justified Type

Betty ran across the street to catch her pet rabbit and was struck by an automobile. Her broken ankle was in a cast for several weeks.

The children in Betty's class wished to do something to make her happy. They decided to make a Book of Surprises for her.

The class divided into groups of three or four to make different parts of the book. One group made riddles and another made games. Others wrote jokes, drew pictures, and wrote or copied poems. Health and safety rules kept a few boys and girls busy, while others made up stories. All these things were talked over by the teacher and the pupils.

❖

"Always look twice when crossing a street."

—Mother

Betty was so happy to get a Book of Surprises from her classmates, it eased the pain of walking around with a big white cast and clunky big crutches. She would read the jokes and the poems when she was feeling sad.

Betty was happy and her rabbit was safe.

Flush Left / Ragged Right Type

Betty ran across the street to catch her pet rabbit and was struck by an automobile. Her broken ankle was in a cast for several weeks.

The children in Betty's class wished to do something to make her happy. They decided to make a Book of Surprises for her.

The class divided into groups of three or four to make different parts of the book. One group made riddles and another made games. Others wrote jokes, drew pictures, and wrote or copied poems. Health and safety rules kept a few boys and girls busy, while others made up stories. All these things were talked over by the teacher and the pupils.

Betty was so happy to get a Book of Surprises from her classmates, it eased the pain of walking around with a big white cast and clunky big crutches. She would read the jokes and the poems when she was feeling sad.

Betty was happy and her rabbit was safe.

"Always look twice when crossing a street."

—Mother

Shapely Text

In fashion, boxy shapes can be disastrous on the wrong figure, but on pages with lots of text, they're très chic. Aligning columns on both the left and right sides creates this square look (called justified type) and is ideal for your primary content.

For other text, like quotes, captions and call-outs, flush left/ragged right or centered formats are good options.

Used in combination, these styles create a nice contrast on the page.

SHOW

One day Mr. Brown Bear met Mr. Sly Fox. Mr. Fox had a string of fish. Mr. Bear wanted some fish also. So they went to the pond and Mr. Fox broke a hole in the ice. He told Mr. Bear that if he would sit with his tail in the hole, he could catch some fish. When the fish bit his tail, he must full it out quickly. Then Mr. Fox ran home to supper.
Mr. Brown Bear sat and sat with his tail in the hole for a long, long time. He grew so tired and hungry that he decided to go home. By that time his tail was frozen into the ice. When he pulled, it snapped off. That is the reason why bears have stubby tails. But it is okay, because they learned to fish with their paws!

Don't let your type get lost in the gutter!

You've Been Framed

Margins act as the frame for the words and images you've assembled. This white space is an important rest for the eyes. Leave a margin around the text with a slightly larger amount along the inside edges, so your words don't end up in the gutter when the book is bound.

For 6" x 9" books, a 1/2" side margin and a 3/4" inside margin gives a good balance of text and space. Larger books, especially landscape, photography or art books, often have margins of 1" or more.

EXTRA CREDIT Want your book to be a little longer? Increase the margins, but don't make them so big that your book looks like an easy reader.

SHOW

Last week, my father bought me a little puppy dog named Monty. He is my best friend. But he has one big problem. He barks. He can't sleep at night. I think he is sick. Yesterday, I called the doctor and he gave him some medicine. It made him sicker than ever, and last night he barked louder than ever. Dad said he was dreaming and

wasn't sick at all. I think he is lonesome for his mother. He is a little puppy and hasn't been away from his mother very long. Today, I put him with another puppy and he hasn't cried at all. Now, both puppies sleep in my bed and I don't sleep at all!

The children of Room Two had a pet show. They brought many pets to school. They brought things for their pets to eat. The teacher said, "Please do not bring any more pets. We cannot take care of so many."

Martha put a big red bow around the neck of her kitty, Millie. Everyone loved the

the big red bow. Millie looked so pretty in her big red bow.

During lunch, all the kids, put ribbons on their pets. They all looked pretty. The teacher said, "Please do not put any more ribbons on your pets, we need to learn to read."

Headers and Footers

Add a professional touch and give the reader a point of reference with headers and footers. They run along the tops and bottoms of the pages and frame the text.

Headers generally list the book title on the upper left side and the chapter title on the upper right. Footers can include the page numbers and the author's name at the bottom.

Look at some books in your genre and you'll see there are lots of variations. Don't sweat it. Choose a style you like and as long as it's used consistently throughout the book, you'll be fine.

DUNCE
I didn't know
a header is on the
top and a footer is
on the bottom!

SHOW

'DO CHICKENS
WEAR STOCKINGS?

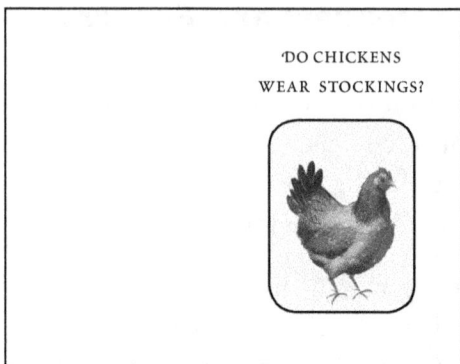

Blank page Chapter opener

☛ *Do not put printed page numbers on blank pages or chapter openers*

One day, Anne went to the barn to feed the chickens. A big hen saw the green spots, which were on Anne's stockings. She thought these spots were something good to eat. She wanted to get them. She tried again and again and again.

Anne said, "Why, you funny old hen. They are not good to eat. Shoo!" Do you think the chicken really wanted to eat Anne's green spotted stockings? Do you think the chicken wanted to wear Anne's green spotted stockings? Do you think chickens ever wear spotted stockings?

Draw a picture of Anne, wearing her green spotted stockings. Now, draw a picture of the chicken wearing green spotted stockings. Which picture looks better?

Take a Number

Page numbers are printed beginning with your first chapter, but that page number can vary. Some authors count chapter one as page one and others start numbering earlier. It's your call.

Even number pages go on the left side of books and odd pages on the right. No exceptions.

EXTRA CREDIT In publishing, page numbers are also called folios.

homework

Pull a few books off your shelf and notice how the pages are numbered before the first chapter starts.

Are they blank, numbered or printed with Roman numerals?

SHOW

How do I tell him blue is a better color?

Cover Shots

Despite what your mother told you, books are completely judged by their covers. Don't put anything on the cover that doesn't help sell your book. Think of it as a first-date outfit that needs to convey both confidence and an engaging personality.

Limit the front cover text to the title, subtitle and author's name, unless you can include an award mention or industry heavyweight blurb. Visuals, if used, should be professional and give the reader a glimpse of what's inside.

If someone likes your front cover, they will most likely flip your book over and check out the back cover. This is your chance to turn browsers into buyers. Good bits to include on the back cover are a summary of the book, a brief author bio and more blurbs by people in your industry.

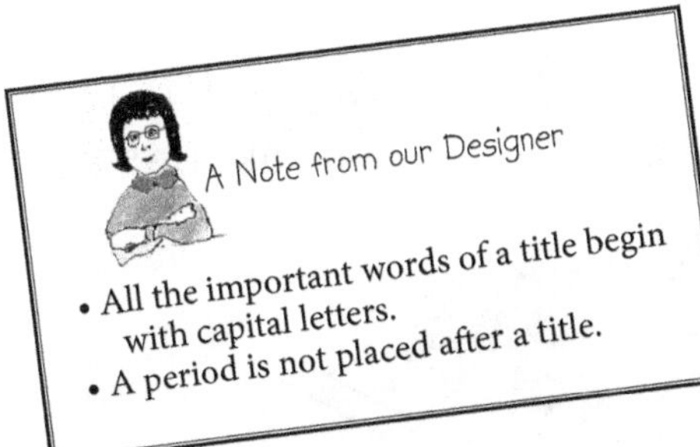

A Note from our Designer
• All the important words of a title begin with capital letters.
• A period is not placed after a title.

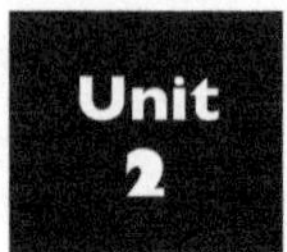

Review: Cut, Paste and Color

Draw a line to the correct size.

Landscape

Square

Vertical

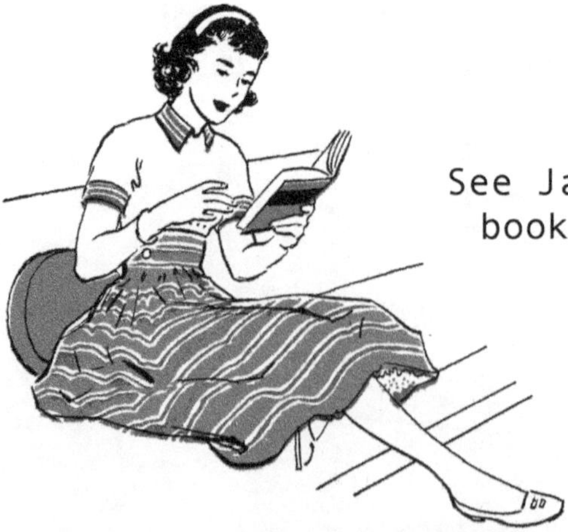

See Jane look at
book designs.

See Dick take a photograph for his book cover.

Write a brief description of each word.

Margins the white space on the top/bottom and sides of the page

Serif type type that have little feet at the end of the strokes

Sans serif type type that does not have little feet at the end of the strokes

Title page the first page of the book with the title, (subtitle if necessary), author and publisher listed

Pick the best cover.

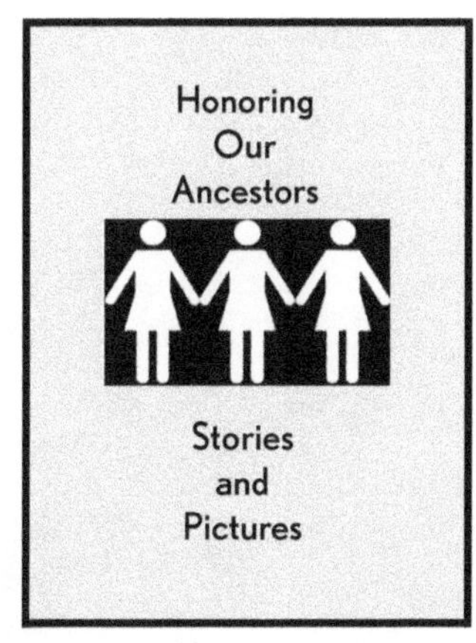

Unit 3

Marketing

Make Some Noise

Your book has been born. Congratulations! (She looks just like you.) Now, who do you plan to send the birth announcement to?

Building your base, developing a tribe, singing to the choir. It doesn't matter what you prefer to call the process of gathering a loyal group of readers; it only matters that you do it. According to Bowker's annual book production report, there were over 3 million new titles by U.S. publishers in 2010, and over 90 percent were on-demand and self-published titles. Of course, your book is better than average, but how do you let people know?

In case you hadn't noticed from the lack of bookstores at the mall, the book landscape has changed dramatically over the past 10 years or so, and that will continue. Most book signings aren't held at bookstores anymore, but rather at hip restaurants, trade shows or as part of a virtual tour. Whether you fully embrace the changes or not, it's important to recognize them and adapt, if you plan to play the game.

Without marketing and promotion, even the best books can be overlooked. Most authors with publishing deals have to do the majority of their own marketing, too, so skip the pity party, self-publishers. The days of turning in an unedited manuscript and waiting for the launch party are long gone.

It's time to swap your author's beret for a hard hat, roll up your sleeves, and get ready to sell some books!

SHOW

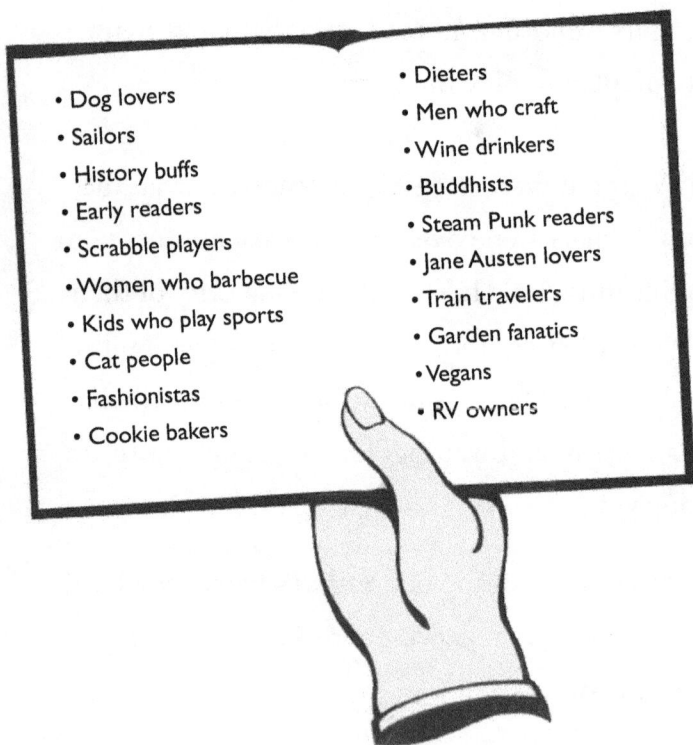

- Dog lovers
- Sailors
- History buffs
- Early readers
- Scrabble players
- Women who barbecue
- Kids who play sports
- Cat people
- Fashionistas
- Cookie bakers
- Dieters
- Men who craft
- Wine drinkers
- Buddhists
- Steam Punk readers
- Jane Austen lovers
- Train travelers
- Garden fanatics
- Vegans
- RV owners

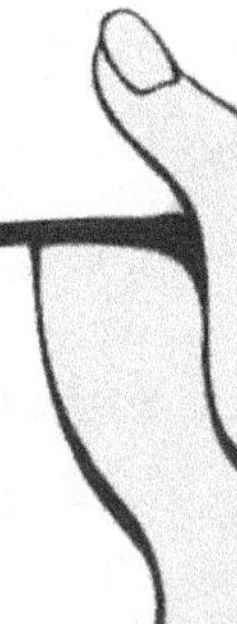

Who are Your Readers?

Close your eyes and picture someone reading your book. Is it a mom grabbing some 'me' time? An urban hipster in a cafe? An attorney on a business flight? Until you have a clear picture of who your readers are, it's hard to know how to reach them.

Thinking everyone will read your book is a lazy (and delusional) strategy. Take the time to figure out who is most likely to buy your book right away and promote to them. They'll tell everyone else.

Keep in mind that it's more effective to think of your readers in terms of their lifestyles instead of categories like age. For instance, dog lovers, moms, foodies and dieters are more descriptive readers than women ages 25 to 54.

Topics for my dog blog

Week 1: Halloween costumes for your dog

Week 2: Discipline strategies

Week 3: Good walking trails for dogs and their owners

Week 4: The best dog food

Week 5: Why dogs are our best friends

Week 6: Tips for taking your dog on vacation

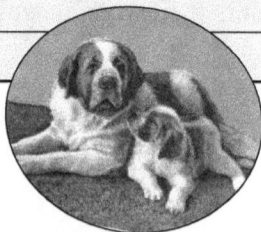

It's All About the Plan

There are lots of options when it comes to promoting your book, so start with a plan to keep track of the timeline and details. The majority of marketing should be done in the three months before and six months after your book is published.

You, the author, are ultimately responsible for ongoing promotion and relationship building, so even if someone else helps you prepare materials, you need to do the footwork to make your plan succeed.

Like most things in life, a few tasks done consistently have more long-term impact than a single grand gesture.

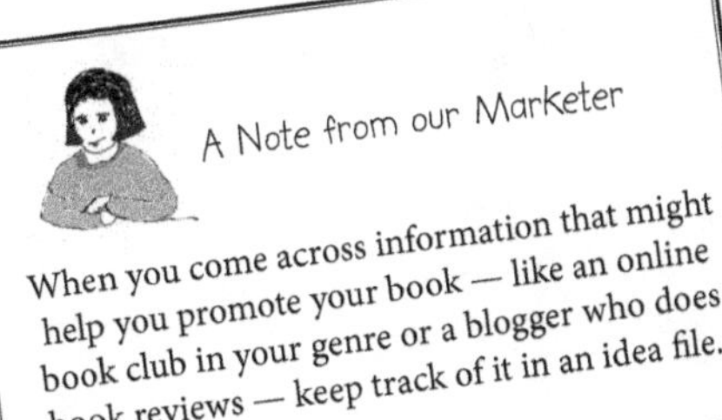

A Note from our Marketer
When you come across information that might help you promote your book — like an online book club in your genre or a blogger who does book reviews — keep track of it in an idea file.

SHOW

What a great review!
Make sure you post it
on your website.
The Best Dog
Book Ever!

Get Found Online

Think you don't need a book website because you have an Amazon page? Think again.

A website (or even a landing page) devoted entirely to your book is base camp for all your other marketing excursions. This is where you build a fire, invite friends and tell the story of your book.

Can a blog be your website? Absolutely. Can a dedicated Facebook page be your website? Sure. The content, and your dedication to keep it current, are more important than the format.

homework

Find 5–10 websites you like (book related or not) and write down what you like about them. Try to include some of these features in your book website.

EXTRA EXTRA

Alert the Press

A press release tells journalists about a newsworthy item. The key is newsworthy. Simply publishing a book doesn't necessarily qualify.

The best way to get the media's attention is to connect your book's topic with a local angle or current news story.

Think like a reporter and figure out what item or trend they might be writing about, and how your expertise can add meaning to their story. For example, a press release for your book about social networking can include ways to use social media while job-hunting in a difficult economy.

Keep your release:

- Short and to the point (one page, please)
- In the third person
- Formatted correctly (find samples online)
- Newsworthy!

Press Kit for *Dogs I Have Known*

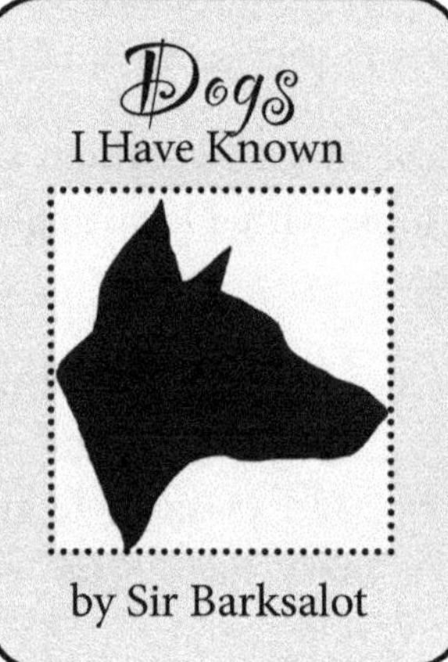
Dogs
I Have Known
by Sir Barksalot

A Synopsis of the book

Images of your book cover and your headshot

Author Bio

Story Angles

Press release

Reviews & awards

The Whole Kit and Caboodle

Along with your press release, create an easy-to-download (PDF) media kit on your website. Having these tools readily available makes the reporter's job a lot easier, and since they're usually on tight deadlines, the odds of them including you in their story go way up.

Contents:

- A synopsis of your book
- Your author bio
- Story angles and/or Q&A that are a good fit for your book's subject matter
- Images of your book cover and your headshot
- Your book-related press release(s)
- Any awards or positive reviews

SHOW

Hello, Queen.
Would you mind
writing the foreword
for my new book?

No problem.
As soon as I walk my
dogs, I will get started.

It's Who You Know

Ask influential people in your field to write a foreword for your book or blurb for the back cover.

Be realistic, professional and polite by preparing easy-to-digest information that doesn't make them work too hard. Send only a synopsis or sample chapter with your request unless they ask to see the entire manuscript.

For blurbs, provide a few samples that someone can tweak, if they're short on time, but still want to help.

Forewords and blurbs have a big influence on your credibility, so try to find at least one or two people who will help your book stand out.

SHOW

The Dog Review
October 12
DOGS • DOGS • DOGS
I just love dogs. I have spent the last 10 years writing about dogs. Some people call me the new Dog Whisperer. Send me your book about dogs. I would love to review it.
About Me

Molly
San Francisco

Blog or Bust

Like publishing, the world of journalism is constantly evolving and blogs are now legitimate contenders. Not every blog, of course. So search out the bloggers who are influential in your book's topic area or are known for reviewing and promoting self-published books.

Type the blog's URL into alexa.com to get information about their traffic and ranking. Read their posts and think about how you can help them, by providing content their readers would enjoy.

When you request a review, let the blogger know you're happy to give them an excerpt to post on their blog or a copy of your book to give away to readers.

DUNCE
I thought bloggers would pay me to talk about my book since it's so good.

SHOW

LinkedIn

YouTube

As seen on the Internet!

Like me on Facebook!

Get Social

Whether you're a Facebook fanatic or not, social media is here to stay and should be part of your book marketing plan. At the very least, secure your name or book title on Facebook and Twitter, so you have the option to connect down the road.

If tweeting and blogging don't come naturally to you, devise a strategy that is authentic but still effective. Write in your own voice and write consistently. It's better to use one or two social media tools on a regular basis and develop relationships, than have a scattered approach.

Start small (update your LinkedIn page to include your book and write one post on your blog every week, for example), and then add other social media tools like Facebook, YouTube and Twitter, if they're a good fit for you.

SHOW

Timing is Everything

Set up interviews and speaking engagements as close to the publication date as possible to start a snowball effect and create awareness with readers.

When your book is new (and therefore news), journalists, bloggers, readers and others pay more attention.

Develop an audience pre-publication by starting a blog, creating a Facebook page and sending an email to your list.

A Note from our Marketer

Do NOT wait months after publication to launch your book. When it is hot off the press — it is hot!

Checklist for getting speaking engagements

Create a flyer that grabs people's attention and gives them a sense of what they'll get out of spending an hour or so with you.

Email a cover letter and link to the PDF flyer on your website (or a hard copy of both) to the person who books speakers at local business groups, churches, community groups, parent associations, book clubs and retailers.

Document speaking success stories, including testimonials from participants and hosts, to help get your foot in the door at larger venues, like colleges and trade shows.

Talk, Talk, Talk

Whether speaking to groups is a dream or a nightmare, you need a strategy for getting in front of people. Old school style includes book signings, talking to local groups, participating in panels and teaching workshops.

Virtual book tours are a hi-tech alternative to get your book and brand in front of thousands (millions?) without leaving your laptop. Also, approach bloggers and online groups about participating in podcasts, webinars and virtual book clubs.

EXTRA CREDIT Create a video of you speaking about your book and post it on your website for instant credibility.

homework

Get a special business card just for your book. Add a line on your card that lets people know you're interested in speaking to their group.

SHOW

You Oughta Be in Pictures

Video is the most viral component of the Internet and authors should take full advantage of its power. If you're not a big name, video lets people get to know (and love) you before, during and after reading your book.

Make sure your script engages readers so they stay tuned and forward your video to others. It doesn't have to be expensive (and shouldn't be longer than a few minutes), but it should showcase your personality and provide a hook that makes people want to know more about your book.

Places to post your video:

- Your book website
- Amazon author page
- YouTube channel
- Blog sites where your book is reviewed

A+

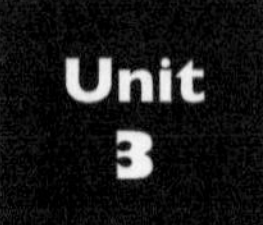

Review: Make Some Noise

How can you let people know you've published a book?

1) Send an email to your list
2) Create a website and write articles linking to it
3) Set up a Facebook page for your book
4) Send a press release to the media
5) Ask book reviewers and bloggers to write about your book
6) Submit your book to book clubs for selection
7) ✔ All of the above

See Dick announce to the world his book is published!

See Jane call Oprah
and ask her to write
her foreword.

Choose the best headline for a book press release.

1) My Book Has Just Been Published!

2) A New Book About Dogs

✔3) San Francisco Native Chronicles City's Dog Craze in New Book, *Dog Tales*

True or False

1) It's best to write my bio in first person. (False)

2) There should be a "Buy" link on every page of my website. (True)

3) Journalists prefer long, detailed emails. (False)

4) When asking people to write blurbs, it's okay to send them a couple of examples. (True)

5) Video is only for famous authors. (False)

Homework

RESOURCES

EDITING AND WRITING

The Associated Press Stylebook, by Associated Press

The Chicago Manual of Style, by University of Chicago Press Staff

The Copyeditor's Handbook, by Amy Einsohn

The Elements of Grammar, by Margaret Shertzer

The Elements of Style, by William Strunk Jr. and E.B. White

Garner's Modern American Usage, by Bryan A. Garner

The New York Times Manual of Style and Usage, by Allan M. Siegal and William G. Connolly

On Writing Well, by William Zinsser

Webster's New World College Dictionary, by Michael E. Agnes

Write Right!: A Desktop Digest of Punctuation, Grammar, and Style, by Jan Venolia

Write That Book Already! The Tough Love You Need to Get Published Now, by Sam Barry and Kathi Kamen Goldmark

RESOURCES

DESIGN

Book Design, by Andrew Haslam

By Its Cover: Modern American Book Cover Design, by Ned Drew and Paul Sternberger

Chip Kidd: Book One: Work: 1986–2006, by Chip Kidd

Graphic Design: The New Basics, by Ellen Lupton and Jennifer Cole Phillips

How to Think Like a Great Graphic Designer, by Debbie Millman

RESOURCES

DESIGN

Layout workbook: A real-world guide to building pages in graphic design, by Kristin Cullen

Making and Breaking the Grid: A Graphic Design Layout Workshop, by Timothy Samara

Pocket Pal: The Handy Little Book of Graphic Arts Production, by Michael H. Bruno

Thinking with Type: A Critical Guide for Designers, Writers, Editors, & Students, by Ellen Lupton

RESOURCES

MARKETING

Book Marketing Buzz: Book Promotion and Publicity Tips for Authors (bookmarketingbuzz.com)

Book Marketing Made Easy: Simple Strategies for Selling Your Nonfiction Book Online, by D'vorah Lansky

The Book Marketing Network: The network for book & ebook authors and publishers (thebookmarketingnetwork.com)

Guerrilla Marketing for Writers: 100 No-Cost, Low-Cost Weapons for Selling Your Work, by Jay Conrad Levinson, Rick Frishman, Michael Larsen and David L. Hancock

Little Spark Media — author videos (littlesparkmedia.com)

The Publicity Hound: Tips, tricks and tools for free publicity (publicityhound.com)

The Well-Fed Self-Publisher: How to Turn One Book into a Full-Time Living, Peter Bowerman (wellfedsp.com)

VOCABULARY

ACKNOWLEDGMENTS — *Think Academy Awards. A place where you thank all the people who have helped you. Don't forget loved ones (or you may be in trouble at home!)*

AUTHOR BIO — *It's all about you. Pull readers in with unique and relevant information about your life and credentials. Create both short (25–50 word) and long (250–500 word) versions and keep it third person, but in a tone that matches your writing style.*

BACK COVER — *Another chance to grab readers by giving them a summary of your book's subject, some blurbs and a brief bio with your photo for added interest.*

VOCABULARY

BAR CODE — *No, this is not a discount at the local tavern. It's a printed image that can be scanned and will tell the world the name, price and ISBN number of your book.*

BLEED — *Art, an image or a color that extends all the way to the top, bottom or sides of your page, leaving no white space. Sometime it bleeds off all four sides.*

BLOG — *Though it sounds like a creature from the black lagoon, blogs (a blend of the words web and log) are actually web pages that tend to be more conversational and interactive, and can be updated frequently. They're not dangerous, but some can be quite frightening.*

BLURB — *Sounds like a hiccup and it sort of is. A short endorsement of your book on the jacket or back cover that can increase sales.*

BUZZ — *The oh-so-pleasing sound of busy bees (readers) talking about your book.*

CENTERED — *Text or images aligned with the middle of the page with an equal amount of white space on each side.*

VOCABULARY

DEDICATION — *A place at the front of your book to honor or praise those who inspired you.*

DINGBAT — *No, not just a brainless twit. A typographical device used decoratively to divide text.*

EBOOK — *Pretty easy … electronic books. The pages never tear and the spine never cracks, although they can run out of juice right at the crucial part of a story.*

FOUR-COLOR PROCESS — *Cyan, Magenta, Yellow and Black (CMYK) are the four colors that are used in color printing.*

VOCABULARY

FONTS — *We won't go into the history of the word font, and what it meant when books were printed on a Gutenberg press. Now, in our digital age, font/typeface are interchangeable.*

FLUSH LEFT/RAGGED RIGHT — *Text that's aligned on the left and with a ragged (but attractive!) texture on the right. Great for captions, sidebars and pull quotes.*

FRONT MATTER — *The first section of a book that includes the foreword, dedication, contents and blank pages. Sometimes numbered in lower-case Roman numerals.*

HALF TITLE PAGE — *A page before the title page, but only listing the title. It can be decorative or simple, and like the title page, always on the right side.*

HORIZONTAL — *What you get when a book bores you into nap time. Also, a book that is wider than it is tall and a great shape for art and photography books.*

VOCABULARY

INTRODUCTION — *A guide that offers a glimpse of your material and your point of view to excite the reader. Just like our mothers told us, it's important to make a good introduction.*

ISBN — *The number assigned to your book to keep track of how many are sold.*

JUSTIFIED TYPE — *Type with straight columns on each side. Easiest to ready and the best choice for most book copy.*

LITERARY — *The writing, study or content of literature that is valued for the quality of the writing. Now, get started!*

MARKETING PLAN — *This evolving document will guide your efforts to promote and sell your book, keep contacts and resources organized and help you shift gears when something isn't working. If you want to sell more books, create a marketing plan!*

VOCABULARY

PAGE COUNT — *The number of pages in the book, even the blank pages. For printing purposes, the total number of pages in your book should be divisable by eight.*

PRESS KIT — *Information that is easy to access and makes it easier for journalists to report on your book. Includes a book synopsis, author bio, story angles or Q&A, book cover and author images, your press release(s) and any awards, quotes by notable people or press coverage received.*

RUNNING FEET — *Also known as footers. Words that run along the bottom of the page and frame the text. Can include the page numbers and the author's name at the bottom.*

RUNNING HEAD — *Also know as headers. Usually with the book title on the upper left side and the chapter title on the upper right, but it can vary.*

VOCABULARY

SPINE — *This edge is what you see when your book is on the shelf. Important information to include: author, title, publisher and publisher's logo. Now stand up straight!*

STORY ANGLE — *Help reporters help you! Come up with a few ideas they could write about that relate to the topic of your book. For example, a book about sugar addiction can be included in stories on diet trends, as well as a story about soda at schools.*

SYNOPSIS — *Short and sweet, a synopsis is a summary of your book that gives readers an idea of what it's about, the genre and your writing style. Useful for your website, press materials, Amazon page and speaking materials.*

TABLE OF CONTENTS — *Lets your reader know how your book is organized and in what order your subjects will appear. All pages are counted, but the front matter before the table of contents is usually not numbered in the contents page.*

VOCABULARY

TITLE PAGE — *The first page of the book with the title, (subtitle if necessary), author and publisher listed.*

TRIM SIZE — *Easy… the size of your book! Most printers have set sizes. Check out their sizes and print prices because a standard 6" X 9" book may be less expensive than a smaller size.*

TYPO — *The goal is to catch these errors before you publish. Includes spelling errors, missed words and double strikes. Editing is key.*

VIRTUAL TOUR — *Pack light! Virtual tours introduce authors and their books to readers via webcam, podcast or phone, where they discuss their book, answer questions and sell books, all from the comfort of home.*

WIDOWS — *Words or short lines at the beginning or end of a paragraph, alone and separated from the rest of the text. Give them a home by adding or deleting words or adjusting the spacing.*

MEET THE TEACHERS

RUTH HAGOPIAN won the esteemed "Readers are Leaders" gold pin award for most books read in Miss Miller's third grade class and hasn't stopped reading since. A positive side effect is that now, errors literally jump off the page as she reads, allowing her to expertly edit memoirs, anthologies, self-help, travel and how-to books with ease. She gives her brain a day off school by perusing art books with lots of pictures.

CATHLEEN O'BRIEN frequently colors outside the lines, despite learning the importance of the grid in graphic design school. She spends countless hours in her design studio, conjuring clever book covers, eradicating widows and perfecting the text-to-white-space ratio.

JULIE THOMPSON started making up stories before she could write, preferring to think of it as a literary exercise, rather than lying. At age 10, after seeing her words in print in the Tulsa Public Schools Sampler, she contracted a writing virus for which there is no cure. In addition to ~~making up stories~~ writing, she enjoys helping other writers shape, edit and market their work and playing euchre.

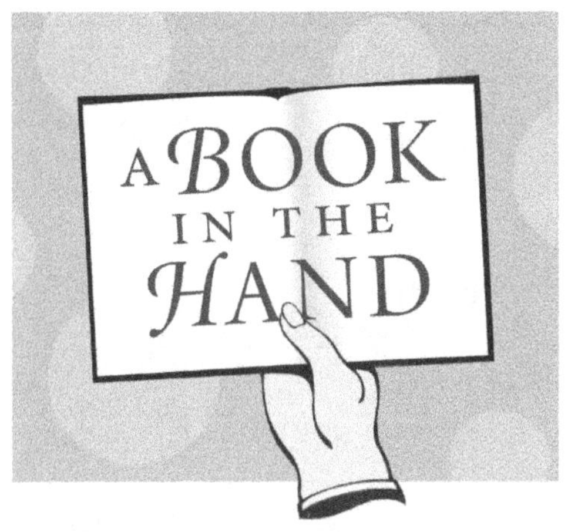

A Book in the Hand *works with individuals, entrepreneurs, nonprofits, small businesses and corporate teams to bring non-fiction book ideas to life. Our team has extensive experience in book layout and design, concept shaping, proposal and manuscript editing, and marketing to give a professional polish to your project. Whether you want to share your expertise with a larger audience, help your business stand out from the crowd or create a memorable client gift, a book helps you tell your story.*

Get that book out of your head and on the page with A Book in the Hand.

YOU DID IT!

A – EXCELLENT
B – GOOD
C – FAIR
U – UNSATISFACTORY
✓ – INDICATES WEAKNESS

	1	2	3	4
WRITING				
ORGANIZATION	A+	A+	A+	A+
TIDY FILES	A+	A+	A+	A+
PERMISSION	A+	A+	A+	A+
ORIGINAL VOICE	A+	A+	A+	A+
EDITING	A+	A+	A+	A+
GRAMMAR	A+	A+	A+	A+
FACT CHECK	A+	A+	A+	A+
DESIGN	A+	A+	A+	A+
SIZE	A+	A+	A+	A+
COLOR	A+	A+	A+	A+
MARKETING	A+	A+	A+	A+
PLAN	A+	A+	A+	A+
WEBSITE	A+	A+	A+	A+
ALERT THE PRESS	A+	A+	A+	A+
EXTRA CREDIT	A+	A+	A+	A+
RESOURCES	A+	A+	A+	A+
VOCABULARY	A+	A+	A+	A+

notes

notes